Continuing Education
Health Informatics 282-002

TABLE OF CONTENTS & ACKNOWLEDGEMENTS

	PAGE
"Chapter 1: The Coding Process" Fletcher, J. ICD-10-CA/CCI Classification Primer, 5th Ed., Fletcher, J. © 2009 Joy Fletcher Reprinted with permission.	1
"Chapter 2: ICD-10-CA" Fletcher, J. ICD-10-CA/CCI Classification Primer, 5th Ed., Fletcher, J. © 2009 Joy Fletcher Reprinted with permission.	7
"Chapter 3: CCI" Fletcher, J. ICD-10-CA/CCI Classification Primer, 5th Ed., Fletcher, J. © 2009 Joy Fletcher Reprinted with permission.	35

Chapter 1

THE CODING PROCESS

- Introduction
- Classification systems
- The coding process
- Purpose of coding

INTRODUCTION

Medical terminology, as it is written by a health care provider to describe a patient's complaint, problem, diagnosis, intervention, or other reason for seeking medical attention, must be translated into a form (numerical codes) which can be easily tabulated, aggregated, and sorted for statistical analysis in an efficient and meaningful manner. Classification systems are designed to fulfill this function. For example, the physician's written diagnosis of "cholelithiasis" translates into the ICD-10-CA diagnosis code of K80.20 *Calculus of gallbladder without cholecystitis*. A diagnosis of "gallstones" also translates into this code. By providing a numerical representation of "cholelithiasis", it is possible to evaluate the care of patients by grouping all patients with a diagnosis stated as cholelithiasis or as gallstones.

CLASSIFICATION SYSTEMS

A classification system is a systematic arrangement of elements within a subject into groups or categories according to pre-established criteria. Classification systems are used in many realms and especially in the sciences. Commonly known examples include the classification of species of plants, birds and animals.

In Canada, there are two classification systems used for data collection within the acute care system: the International Statistical Classification of Diseases and Related Health Problems Tenth Revision, Canada (ICD-10-CA) and the Canadian Classification of Health Interventions (CCI). These two classification systems are the focus of this text. These are sometimes described as the classification standards for data collection in Canada and are not to be confused with the Canadian Coding Standards, a companion document that supports the application of ICD-10-CA and CCI in Canada.

ICD-10-CA is based on ICD-10, which is developed and maintained by the World Health Organization, and modified for use in Canada by the Canadian Institute for Health Information (CIHI). The elements being arranged are diseases, injuries and other reasons for contact with the health care system. ICD-10-CA is described in detail in Chapter 2.

The CCI was developed by CIHI. The elements being arranged in the CCI are interventions such as diagnostic or therapeutic procedures. CCI is described in detail in Chapter 3.

THE CODING PROCESS

The coding process is a much more complex function than merely assigning a number from a classification system to a term. The coding process contains two distinct, but related components:

1. Interpretation of the source documents, and
2. Code assignment.

INTERPRETATION OF THE SOURCE DOCUMENTS

Medical terminology describing the reason for a patient's encounter appears on a source document. Examples of source documents are inpatient records, same day surgery records, emergency reports and ambulatory care reports. Source documents vary significantly between facilities, and between health care providers within facilities. Frequently the documentation is as unique as the patients themselves.

The interpretation of the source documents is, by far, the most challenging component of the coding process. It requires a thorough review of all documentation within a record to obtain the detailed information required for accurate code assignment. For example, a diagnostic statement of "fractured wrist" requires a review of the reports of the physical examination and the x-ray to obtain the specific information necessary for classification, such as the bone involved, the particular part of the bone and the type of fracture.

Interpretation of the source document requires a thorough understanding of medical terminology, anatomy, pathophysiology and health care interventions. This understanding is critical to completely and accurately capture all the factors pertinent to an episode of care and to determine the significance of a condition in the current episode of care. For example, in the case of a patient with both a renal condition and diabetes, accurate and complete classification requires determination of such details as the type of diabetes, whether the diabetes is poorly controlled, the nature of the renal disease, symptoms of the diseases, related complications, and the impact of both conditions on resource usage.

Differences in interpretation of the source documents is, perhaps, the most significant factor contributing to variance in encoded data. This variance in interpretation is influenced by physician documentation styles, the completeness of the record at the time of coding, and coder knowledge and experience.

CODE ASSIGNMENT

Code assignment involves selecting and assigning alphanumeric codes from the classification systems to represent diagnostic and intervention data. Accurate code assignment requires interpretation and application of:
- the classification systems, coding instructions, guidelines, conventions,
- standards, rules, policies and
- professional ethics.

The classification systems contain numerous and various instructions, guidelines and conventions that are communicated via its structure and presentation, in notes, or by the use of special symbols and punctuation. These might be found at the beginning of the classification itself, at the beginning of chapters, or in various places throughout. It is incumbent on the coder to remember where these are located, what they mean, understand how they are applied and, of course, apply them accurately. The challenge to accuracy and consistency in coding arises when individual coders apply these factors to the often unique circumstances recorded in each patient record.

National standards, provincial/territorial rules and local policies are designed to enable consistency in data collection and for the provision of meaningful and reliable data while balancing the burden of data collection. National standards also provide direction to support consistent interpretation of the classification systems, and their instructions, guidelines and conventions. The coder must keep abreast of changes. Strict adherence to national, provincial/ territorial and local standards, policies and rules is necessary for coding consistency. However, the coder must be able to identify when these conflict and follow up appropriately.

Coders must ensure that the information captured in code accurately reflects the information recorded in the patient record. Good professional ethics are necessary to ensure code assignment decisions are not influenced by their impact on various uses of the data, such as reimbursement and patient care quality indicators.

PURPOSE OF CODING

The purpose of coding is to provide health care data that can be stored, indexed, and easily retrieved. The encoded data can be aggregated, tabulated and sorted for statistical analysis and reporting, or it can be used to analyze individual cases and facilitate access to the individual patient record.

STATISTICAL USES
Numerous agencies and organizations analyze encoded data to study and report on a variety of aspects of health, health care and factors that influence health. In Canada, this includes Statistics Canada, the Public Health Agency of Canada (PHAC), Health Canada, CIHI, provincial and territorial ministries of health and a variety of special interest groups. Use of the data for these purposes is described as secondary use. Some examples of statistical uses of encoded health care data include:

Etiology and Incidence of Disease
Epidemiologists, government ministries of health, public health agencies, community planners and occupational health professionals may use encoded data to study frequency of disease, identify at-risk populations based on specific demographic, diagnostic or environmental factors and inform public policy decisions.

Resource Allocation and Management
Agencies responsible for the funding and provision of health care such as government ministries of health, insurers and health care administrators may use encoded data to review caseloads, determine specialty needs, establish staffing requirements, manage patient scheduling, manage the utilization of resources, prioritize service delivery, identify needs and allocate resources. These data are often reported in the form of statistical indicators.

Managing the Quality and Safety of Health Care
Peer reviewers, credentialing bodies and health care managers may use encoded data to evaluate the quality of care rendered, assess safety aspects of care, measure outcome of care and make recommendations for improvement. These data are also frequently reported in the form of statistical indicators.

Research
Researchers use encoded data to develop medical knowledge, to evaluate treatment options and protocols, and to develop new advances in medical science.

Establishing Funding Rates
Payors such as government agencies and insurance companies use aggregated data to establish funding rates.

INDIVIDUAL USES
Some examples of individual uses include:

Reimbursement
Encoded data may be used on an individual basis as a means to establish reimbursement for out-of-province claims, workers' compensation claims, and other insurance claims.

Education
Encoded data provides a means of access to the documentation of specific cases by educators and students to enhance the learning process in the medical, nursing and allied health fields of study.

Research
Encoded data permits access to specific types of records (e.g. all records of patients having a craniotomy) to obtain detail not routinely collected.

Complete Exercise 1.1

Chapter 1 — Exercise 1.1

THE CODING PROCESS

Suggested activities:

① Read Chapter 1.

② Identify three topics contained in the reading material which you would like to discuss or for which you would like further clarification. Formulate three questions relating to these topics.

③ Identify three key points from this chapter which are essential for the coder to remember.

④ Search the library or the internet to find three to five examples of statistical uses of encoded health care data. Include examples of statistical indicator reporting or public policy decisions that would have been informed by health data.

⑤ Discuss your questions, key points and findings in class or with a certified health information manager.

Chapter 2

ICD-10-CA

- Introduction
- General principles of ICD-10-CA
- Structure and presentation of ICD-10-CA
- Locating codes in ICD-10-CA
- General coding guidelines

INTRODUCTION

ICD-10-CA is the *International Classification of Diseases and Health-Related Problems Tenth Revision, Canada*. It is a Canadian modification of the ICD-10 which was adopted by the World Health Assembly in 1990 and published by the World Health Organization (WHO) in 1993. ICD-10 is the most recent revision of the international classification for classifying mortality and morbidity data used throughout the world. Statistics Canada and provincial vital statistics agencies use the ICD-10, as produced by WHO, for mortality applications. ICD-10-CA is used to collect morbidity data. The Canadian modifications to ICD-10 were made to permit specific capture of conditions and external factors contributing to disease and injury that are of importance to Canadian ministries of health, health care agencies and researchers. For example, modifications were made to cardiovascular codes to capture greater detail about cardiac conditions and external factor codes were expanded to permit capture of accidents relating to skis, skates and other ice and snow paraphernalia. Other countries which have undertaken modifications to ICD-10 include Australia and the United States.

ICD-10-CA is produced for use in Canada by the Canadian Institute for Health Information (CIHI) under a license agreement from WHO. CIHI is an independent, not-for-profit organization mandated jointly by federal and provincial/territorial ministers to provide relevant, objective, accurate and timely health information.

ICD-10-CA and the *Canadian Classification of Health Interventions* (CCI) have been adopted in Canada as the exclusive national standards for diagnosis and intervention classification beginning April 1, 2001. They are published on a CD-ROM in a software application called *FAST Folio Views®* by Newbook Production Inc. Open this software to follow along with this discussion.

A companion document the *Canadian Coding Standards for Version 2009 ICD-10-CA and CCI* is published by CIHI in Adobe portable document format (PDF) and available for download from the CIHI website. These Standards are a compilation of the international rules of coding as established by the World Health Organization (ICD-10, Volume 2), diagnosis typing standards developed by CIHI to denote case complexity in Canadian facilities, and other directives developed to promote consistency in classification to meet Canadian reporting needs.

Previous versions of ICD lacked an updating mechanism to accommodate the classification of new diseases and new medical knowledge. Changes were not made to the classification until entirely new editions were released, which was approximately every 10 years. WHO has provided updates to ICD-10 annually since 1996. In 2004, a second edition of ICD-10 was published which included the updates that came into effect from 1996–2003 and a new code for severe acute respiratory syndrome (SARS). CIHI incorporates ICD-10 amendments into ICD-10-CA and has developed an update process for both the ICD-10-CA and the CCI, releasing new versions to these classification systems on a triennial basis. Interim errata and addenda may be produced between versions and it is imperative that users ensure these are applied.

The CCI is described in Chapter 3.

GENERAL PRINCIPLES OF ICD-10-CA

ICD-10-CA is a statistical classification system. A classification is a systematic method of arranging elements based on a particular point of view. For example, physicians look at health care conditions and problems from the point of view of medical diagnoses. Health care providers engaged in rehabilitation view health conditions and problems in terms of functionality or disabilities and impairments. The nursing profession looks at health care conditions and problems in relation to specific care needs. The arrangement of elements in ICD-10-CA is based on the physician point of view, i.e. diseases, injuries and health related problems as described in medical diagnoses.

As a statistical classification, ICD-10-CA is confined to a limited number of mutually exclusive categories. In other words, it provides for one, and only one, category for each and every possible disease or morbid condition. The categories in ICD-10-CA have been chosen to facilitate the statistical study of disease phenomena. A disease entity that is of particular public health importance or one that occurs frequently is assigned its own, very specific category. Less specific categories may contain groups of separate, but related conditions. Since every disease or morbid condition must have a place in the classification, residual (i.e. catch-all) categories for other less specific, less common and miscellaneous conditions are provided. For example, cleft lip and cleft palate are congenital anomalies that occur frequently enough, and are of particular public interest, that separate categories are provided for these (Q35–Q37 *Cleft lip and cleft palate*). However, a cleft of the thyroid cartilage is not particularly common, and is classified to the residual category of Q31.8 *Other congenital malformations of larynx* which includes anomalies of the cricoid cartilage, epiglottis, glottis, larynx and thyroid cartilage.

This concept of grouping related conditions into categories is what distinguishes a statistical classification from a nomenclature. A nomenclature provides a separate category for each and every known disease or morbid condition.

AXIS
Axis is the criterion on which the classification is based. The ICD-10-CA is a variable-axis classification. The primary axes on which this classification are based are:
- epidemic diseases
- constitutional or general diseases
- local diseases arranged by site
- developmental diseases
- injuries

Within these primary arrangements, secondary axes can be found. Table 2.1 provides examples of axes used in the classification.

| EXAMPLES OF AXES USED IN ICD-10-CA ||||
ICD-10-CA Code	Translation	Primary Axis	Secondary Axis
J15.1	Pneumonia due to Pseudomonas	Local Disease by Site (Respiratory System)	Etiology (organism)
D01.0	Carcinoma in situ of colon	General Disease (Neoplasia)	Anatomical site (colon)
C81.2	Hodgkin's disease mixed cellularity	General Disease (Neoplasia)	Morphology (mixed cellularity)
G40.00	Localization-related (focal)(partial) idiopathic epilepsy and epileptic syndromes with seizures of localized onset, not stated as intractable	Local Disease by Site (Nervous System)	Clinical manifestation (type of seizure) and severity (intractability)
G41.0	Grand mal status epilepticus	Local Disease by Site (Nervous System)	Severity
J45.01	Predominantly allergic asthma with stated status asthmaticus	Local Disease by Site (Respiratory System)	Etiology (allergic) and severity

Table 2.1

STRUCTURE AND PRESENTATION OF ICD-10-CA

ICD-10-CA contains two major components:

1. **Tabular List**
   This is the classification itself. It consists of a numeric listing in code number order of diagnosis codes, injury codes and codes describing other reasons for contact with the health care system.
2. **Alphabetical Index**
   This is an alphabetical listing of diseases, conditions, and injuries leading to the codes in the tabular list.

The ICD-10-CA tabular list is organized by **chapters**, **blocks**, and **categories**. This can be revealed by looking at the table of contents in ICD-10-CA which can be revealed by clicking on the contents tab and then the plus sign at the beginning of the listing.

CHAPTERS

There are 23 chapters, most of which are developed from the primary axes of the classification and are described in Table 2.2.

The first two and the last two of the groups listed in Table 2.2 represent special group chapters, while the other group (local diseases arranged by site) represents chapters commonly referred to as body system chapters. In general, conditions are primarily classified to one of the special group chapters. Where there is any doubt as to where a condition should be classified, the special group chapters take priority. [ICD-10, Vol 2, p16]

PRIMARY AXIS OF CERTAIN CHAPTERS IN ICD-10-CA		
Chapters	Primary Axis	Chapter Type
I	Epidemic diseases	Special group
II – V	Constitutional or general diseases	Special group
VI – XIV	Local diseases arranged by site	Body system
XV – XVII	Developmental diseases	Special group
XIX	Injuries	Special group

Table 2.2

Example:

Carcinoma of sigmoid colon.	C18.7 Malignant neoplasm of sigmoid colon **not** K63.88 Other specified diseases of intestine (small)(large)

Example:

Acute chlamydia cystitis.	A56.0 Chlamydia infection of lower genitourinary tract **not** N30.0 Acute cystitis

> When a condition can be classified to both a special group chapter and a body system chapter, choose the code from the special group chapter.

Additional chapters which fall outside the descriptions of the primary axes are:
- Chapter XVIII Symptoms, signs and abnormal clinical and laboratory findings, not elsewhere classified (R00-R99)
- Chapter XX External causes of morbidity and mortality (V01-Y98)
- Chapter XXI Factors influencing health status and contact with health services (Z00-Z99)
- Chapter XXII Morphology of neoplasms
- Chapter XXIII Provisional codes for research and temporary assignment.

These chapters provide detail important for research and evaluation of the use of health care resources. They include information such as undiagnosed conditions and external causes of injury (e.g. motor vehicle accident).

The first character of an ICD-10-CA code is an alphabetic letter and each letter is associated with a particular chapter. Smaller chapters may share a letter (e.g. D and H) and large chapters may require more than one letter (e.g. Chapters I, II, XIX and XX). The letter "U" is reserved for codes for research purposes and for temporary placement of newly-created categories until a permanent placement is determined.

Important information is provided at the beginning of all chapters. Coders must review these instructions prior to confirming their selection of a code from the chapter to ensure accurate code assignment.

> To ensure accurate code assignment, coders must review instructions at the beginning of a chapter before confirming their selection of a code from the chapter.

BLOCKS

The chapters are subdivided into blocks of three-character categories. A block groups together one or more adjacent categories into a related group of diagnoses. In the scheme of the classification, a block represents a level of grouping between chapters and categories. Expanding a chapter in the table of contents (using a mouse, click on the '+' sign) reveals the blocks in the chapter. Examples of blocks are:
- D50–D53 Nutritional anaemias
- N60–N64 Disorders of breast.

Important information is also provided at the beginning of blocks. Coders must review these instructions prior to confirming their selection of a code from a block to ensure accurate code assignment.

> To ensure accurate code assignment, coders must review instructions at the beginning of a block before confirming their selection of a code from the block.

THREE-CHARACTER CATEGORIES

Categories within each chapter are represented by three characters: an alphabetic character followed by two numeric characters. A three-character category may represent either a group of closely related conditions or a single disease entity (i.e. conditions that warrant their own category because of their frequency, severity or susceptibility to public health intervention). Not all available three-character categories have been used, allowing space for future revision and expansion (e.g. N65 and Q29).

There is usually provision for "other" conditions and "unspecified" conditions which cannot be classified in the preceding categories. This allows for many different but rarer conditions, as well as unspecified conditions (i.e. insufficient documentation to assign the condition to a more specific category) to be included in the classification. The "other" and "unspecified" categories are referred to as **residual categories**. Examples of residual categories include:
- N28 *Other disorders of kidney and ureter, not elsewhere classified* is an example of an "other" three-character category
- N23 *Unspecified renal colic* is an example of an "unspecified" three-character category.

Most three-character categories are further subdivided into four-character categories. Where this is the case, the fourth digit is mandatory; the three-character code cannot stand alone. In ICD-10-CA and in this text, the ".–" (point dash) symbol is used to indicate an incomplete ICD-10-CA code. When the three-character category has not been further subdivided, the three-character code stands alone (e.g. N40 *Hyperplasia of prostate*).

> When a category has been further subdivided, assign all possible characters. Use a three-character code only when the category has not been further subdivided.

Important information is provided at the beginning of three-character categories. Coders must review these instructions prior to confirming their selection of a code from a category to ensure accurate code assignment.

> To ensure accurate code assignment, coders must review instructions at the beginning of each three-character category before confirming their selection of a code from the category.

FOUR-CHARACTER SUBCATEGORIES
Four-character subcategories are used to provide more detailed information within a three-character category. When the three-character category is for a single disease, the fourth character may represent different sites or extent of the condition (e.g. K35.– *Acute appendicitis*). When the three-character category represents a group of conditions, the fourth character may describe individual diseases within the group (e.g. I78.– *Diseases of capillaries*).

The fourth character .8 is generally used for "other" conditions within the three-character category and .9 is used to represent the three-character category without further specification (i.e. "unspecified" conditions). Examples of these **residual subcategories** at the fourth character level include:
- N64.8   Other specified disorders of breast
- N64.9   Disorder of breast, unspecified.

FIFTH- AND SIXTH-CHARACTER SUBCATEGORIES
The fifth- and sixth-character levels provide subclassifications to represent an additional axis. Residual subcategories may also be found at this level. Examples of fifth and sixth character subcategories can be found in:
- Chapter XIII *Diseases of the musculoskeletal system and connective tissue (M00–M99)* where the fifth-character subcategories indicate anatomical site
- Chapter XV *Pregnancy, childbirth and the puerperium (O00–O99)* where the sixth-character subcategories indicate episode of care.

Complete Exercise 2.1

LOCATING CODES IN ICD-10-CA

THE ALPHABETICAL INDEX
The alphabetical index is an alphabetical listing of diseases, conditions, injuries and factors influencing health status and contact with health services which leads to the codes in the tabular list. It is an extensive list of diagnostic terms typically found in health care documentation. It contains more inclusion terms than the tabular list and for this reason, must always be referenced first before proceeding to the tabular list.

> The alphabetical index must always be referenced first before proceeding to the tabular list.

The alphabetical index consists of three sections:
- Section I–*Alphabetical Index to Diseases and Nature of Injuries* is the index to codes in all chapters in the tabular list **excluding** Chapter XX *External causes of morbidity and mortality (V01-Y98)* and some of Chapter XIX *Injury, poisoning and certain other consequences of external causes (S00-T98)*. Section I can be accessed by selecting the index query button (binoculars #1). A table is used within this section to assist in locating the correct codes for neoplasms. The neoplasm table can be accessed directly by selecting binoculars #5.
- Section II–*External Causes of Injury* is the index to most of the codes in the tabular list in Chapter XX. It can be accessed by selecting the external causes query button (binoculars #2).
- Section III–*Table of Drugs and Chemicals* is the index to the remaining codes in Chapters XIX and XX relating to drugs and chemicals. It can be accessed by selecting the table of drugs query button (binoculars #3).

The alphabetical index is organized by lead terms with secondary terms indented below each lead term. **Lead terms** indicate the noun expressed as the name of a disease, injury or other pathological condition. **Secondary terms** are the adjectives and are described as "modifiers". They refer to anatomical site, the variety or type of the disease or injury, etiology, or other special circumstances. For example, in "acute appendicitis", "appendicitis" is the noun and, therefore, the lead term and "acute" is the adjective and, therefore, the secondary term. To locate "acute appendicitis" in the alphabetical index:

1. Click on the alphabetical index search button (binoculars #1).

2. Enter "appendicitis" in the space provided for the lead term. Notice the **word wheel** to the left in the window. Use this to identify alternate spellings or forms of words. You can click on words in the word wheel to drop them into the lead term or secondary term fields.

3. Enter "acute" in the space provided for the secondary term.

4. Select "ok". This takes you to the spot in the alphabetical index where appendicitis is the lead term and acute is the secondary term.

Lead terms are listed in bold lettering. Secondary terms are listed beneath lead terms and are preceded by a hyphen. They are listed in alphabetical order with the exception of the lead term "with" which is listed first. When secondary terms can be further specified, the additional modifiers are indented below the secondary term and preceded by another hyphen. This indentation may be applied several times to accommodate the degree of specificity as necessary, such that it is possible for a specific secondary term to be preceded by six hyphens (or more). For example:

Hepatitis
- viral
- - type
- - - B
- - - - with
- - - - - delta-agent
- - - - - - with hepatic coma B16.0

Following each term in the alphabetical index is the likely code to which the condition is classified in the tabular list. In the acute appendicitis example the code K35.8 (in hypertext) is provided. This code is not assigned without making reference back to the tabular list (by clicking on the code itself) and reviewing its instructional notes, inclusion and exclusion notes, and supplemental information to ensure that the code is complete and fits with the circumstances in the source documents. Remember that these notes are found at the beginning of the chapter, block, three-character category and the code itself.

Sometimes the alphabetical index will supply a partial code in which a missing digit is identified by a dash (e.g. Z86.–) and other times the missing digits are not identified by a dash (e.g. O26.8). In both cases the coder must go to the tabular list to complete the code.

> Never assign codes directly from the alphabetical index. Always refer to the tabular list to review all inclusion and exclusion notes and supplemental information.

Secondary terms are also called **essential modifiers**. These terms, or their synonyms, must be present in the documentation before the code following them can be assigned. Lead terms and secondary terms are sometimes followed by additional terms in parentheses. In the acute appendicitis example there are several terms in parentheses following the secondary term "acute". These are called **nonessential modifiers**. The presence or absence of these terms in the source document does not affect code selection.

Not all search terms are as readily located as acute appendicitis. A search on the lead term "pregnancy" reveals several hits. The first hit will not necessarily be the hit you are looking for. You must step through each hit using the **"next partition hit" icon** (small double arrows pointing to the right) until you come to the place in the index where "pregnancy" is the first word at the margin, i.e. the lead term. The same applies for secondary terms. For example, search for "Klebsiella pneumonia". The lead term is "pneumonia" and the secondary term is "Klebsiella". You must step through the secondary terms using the **"next hit" icon** (large double arrows pointing to the right) until you come to the place in the index where "Klebsiella" is the first indented term preceded by only one hyphen. The top window in the Folio software, called the reference window, provides a **breadcrumb trail** to demonstrate placement within the alphabetical index.

> Use the small double arrow button (next partition icon) to step from lead term to lead term.
> Use the large double arrow button (next hit icon) to step from subterm to subterm within a lead term.

When a lead term cannot be found in the alphabetical index, the coder must think of synonymous or alternate terms to locate the condition. For example, there is no lead term for "zit". If the term was used to mean "pimple", enter "pimple" as the lead term. (It is unlikely one would ever come across this term in health care documentation, but it makes the point!)

In some circumstances the disease condition may be described in adjectival form. For example, in "ectopic kidney", the disease condition is described as an adjective (ectopic). Sometimes the alphabetical index lists both the adjective and the noun form of the disease condition (e.g. ectopic, ectopia), but often only the noun form is found and the coder must convert adjectival statements into a noun. For example, deranged joint must be converted to derangement, joint. When all synonyms and alternate terms have been exhausted, the last resort is to reference the lead terms of "Disease", "Disorder", or "Abnormality"; the secondary term is the anatomical site. Alternatively the lead term can be left blank and a search conducted on a secondary term only.

> When you cannot find a lead term in the alphabetical index and have exhausted all alternative terms, leave the lead term blank and conduct a search on a secondary term only.

The coder must also consider synonyms and alternate terms when a secondary term cannot be located under a lead term. When a condition is described specifically, but no secondary term can be located, the coder must look for the secondary term "**specified NEC**" (not elsewhere classified). In confirming this code selection in the tabular list, the coder must review the code title, inclusion notes, exclusion notes, the subcategories within the three-digit category, and any other instructions. Assignment of a "specified NEC" category implies the documentation has described the person's condition in specific terms, but the classification does not provide a separate specific code for the condition. For example, the physician describes the patient's condition as "acne papulosa". There is no secondary term for "papulosa" under the lead term of "acne". In this case, the coder must consider all synonyms and alternate terms for "papulosa" and when this fails, the coder must look for the secondary term "specified NEC". This directs the coder to classify this case to *L70.8 Other acne*. On confirming this code selection in the tabular list, a review of the code title, inclusion notes, exclusion notes and other subcategories within L70.– *Acne* do not indicate that a specific fourth character applies for acne papulosa, thus L70.8 is the correct code.

> Use "specified NEC" as the secondary term when a specific term used in the documentation is not listed as a secondary term and the term cannot be assigned to a synonymous term.

The code following the lead term in the alphabetical index represents the residual category of "unspecified" or "**NOS**" (not otherwise specified). Before selecting this code, the coder must review all secondary terms to determine whether a more specific code might apply. When a more specific term cannot be located, the coder tentatively selects the code following the lead term and then carefully reviews the code title, inclusion notes, exclusion notes, other codes within the three-digit category and any other instructions in the tabular list to determine whether a more specific code can be assigned. Assignment of an unspecified category usually implies that the documentation does not provide the specific information concerning the person's condition to permit assignment of a more specific code.

> Use "unspecified" or "NOS" categories only when the documentation does not provide the detail needed to assign the condition to a more specific category. Before selecting an unspecified category, carefully review the:
> - code title,
> - inclusion notes at all levels,
> - exclusions notes at all levels,
> - other codes within the three-digit category,
> - any other instruction in the tabular.

Sometimes the alphabetical index provides more than one code following a lead term or a subterm:
- When two codes are supplied and one of them is an asterisk code, both codes must be assigned. This convention is explained in the next section of this chapter under the heading, *Dual Classification*.
- Sometimes two codes are contained in parentheses and separated by a slash (/). This also means that both codes are assigned. This convention is explained in the next section of this chapter under the heading *"Use Additional Code" or "Code Separately" Instruction*.
- When more than one code is provided with no separation or symbols, the coder must look each code up in the tabular list to select the one that is most appropriate for the circumstances of the case. To see an example of this, conduct a search for diabetic coma.

The coder must look at each of the codes E10.0, E11.0, E13.0 and E14.0 to select the most appropriate category. This convention is often used for conditions relating to diabetes.

For more information on using the alphabetical index, read the section in the ICD-10-CA entitled *Conventions Used in the Alphabetical index*. You can locate this by opening the table of contents and double clicking on this text. Pay particular attention to the warning under *Abbreviation NEC*.

Complete Exercise 2.2

THE TABULAR LIST

To reiterate, once a tentative code has been selected from the alphabetical index, it must be verified in the tabular list by reviewing its instructional notes, inclusion and exclusion notes and supplemental information to ensure that the code is complete and fits with the circumstances in the source documents. These notes are found at the:

- code itself,
- beginning of a category,
- beginning of the block and
- beginning of the chapter.

The interpretation of **excludes notes** can be confusing. Terms listed as excluded terms are not classified to that category. However, you are not prevented from assigning an additional code to describe the excluded term as long as it provides useful information and the terms in question are not mutually exclusive.

Example:

Rectal fistula to skin and to vagina.	K60.4	Rectal fistula
The excludes note at K60.4 is interpreted to mean that the coder must not assign K60.4 to describe a rectovaginal fistula. However, when the patient has both a rectovaginal fistula and a fistula from the rectum to the skin, both codes are assigned as the conditions are not mutually exclusive and it is important to identify each.	N82.3	Fistula of vagina to large intestine

Example:

Diverticulitis of the ileum and colon with abscess and perforation.	K57.4	Diverticular disease of both small and large intestine with perforation and abscess
The excludes note at K57.0 *Diverticular disease of small intestine with perforation and abscess* means that when both the large and small bowel are involved in disease, a combination code is provided. It is redundant to assign both codes, i.e. it is not useful information.		

Example:

Congenital diaphragmatic hernia.	Q79.0	Congenital diaphragmatic hernia
The exclude note at K44 *Diaphragmatic hernia* means that this code is not assigned if the hernia is congenital. These conditions are mutually exclusive and only one or the other code can be assigned.		

Example:

Peripheral neuritis complicating pregnancy (patient is discharged undelivered).	O26.803	Other specified pregnancy-related conditions, antepartum condition or complication
	G62.9	Polyneuropathy, unspecified

The alphabetical index leads to O26.8. This reflects the hierarchical nature of ICD-10-CA in which special group chapters take priority. This is reinforced by excludes notes at the beginning of chapters. At the beginning of Chapter VI - *Diseases of the nervous system (G00-G99)* there is an excludes note advising that when nervous system conditions complicate pregnancy the condition is classified to O00–O99. There is also an excludes note at the beginning of the block *Polyneuropathies and other disorders of the peripheral nervous system (G60-G64)*. These excludes notes mean the primary code must be O26.8. However, they do not prevent the assignment of G62.9 to distinguish peripheral neuritis from other inclusions at O26.8. It adds useful information and is not mutually exclusive.

There are certain other instructional notes, abbreviations, and conventions, used in the tabular list that are important for the coder to understand. These are described in the section in the ICD-10-CA entitled *Conventions Used in the Tabular List of Diseases*. You can locate this by opening the table of contents and double clicking on this text.

Complete Exercise 2.3

GENERAL CODING GUIDELINES

The alphabetical index contains many terms not included in the tabular list. Accurate coding requires that both the index and the tabular list be consulted prior to code assignment. There are certain other principles of classification and coding that must be understood for accurate code assignment.

> Consult both the alphabetical index and the tabular list when searching for ICD-10-CA codes.

USE OF COMBINATION CODES AND MULTIPLE CODES

All conditions which affect the care, influence the health status and treatment of the patient, or are the reason for treatment during an encounter are coded. In other words, when a condition is relevant to the current episode of care, it must be coded. In many circumstances where there is a relationship between conditions, ICD-10-CA provides either a combination category, a dual classification, a "use additional code" instruction or a "code separately" instruction. When these features are not provided, the coder may need to assign more than one code to fully describe a patient's condition. Multiple codes are also required when a patient presents with two or more unrelated conditions impacting the episode of care.

When multiple codes are required to describe a condition, the one code that describes the most fundamental aspect of the condition, usually the etiology, is described as the primary code. It is the code the classification considers mandatory in applications where only a single code can be assigned (e.g. in mortality coding). There are some blocks and categories in ICD-10-CA that contain a note indicating the codes that cannot be used in primary coding. One example where this note can be found is at the beginning of the block *Bacterial, viral and other infectious agents* (B95–B97). Another example is at the beginning of the category R65 *Systemic inflammatory response syndrome [SIRS]*. This means these codes cannot be used alone and must follow another code from the classification to indicate the underlying condition.

Combination Categories

A combination code is a single code that classifies two conditions or a diagnosis with an associated secondary process (manifestation) or complication. In other words, there is a relationship between two conditions. Combination codes are usually located in the alphabetical index under secondary terms such as "with", "due to", "in" and "complicating". Only the combination code is assigned when it fully identifies the diagnostic conditions involved.

Example:

Influenza with pneumonia.	J11.0 Influenza with pneumonia, virus not identified

Dual Classification

ICD-10-CA provides a dual classification for circumstances when there are two codes for diagnostic statements containing information about both an underlying generalized disease and a manifestation in a particular organ or site which is a clinical problem in its own right. The primary code is for the underlying disease and is marked with a dagger (†). The manifestation code is marked with an asterisk (*). Both codes must be assigned; the dagger code is always sequenced before the asterisk code. The asterisk code may never be used alone. Both the dagger and asterisk code are provided in the alphabetical index and are usually located under the connecting words "in", "due to" or "with", or under an adjective for the underlying condition.

Example:

Mumps orchitis.	B26.0 † Mumps orchitis N51.1 * Disorders of testis and epididymis in diseases classified elsewhere

"Use Additional Code" or "Code Separately" Instruction

Sometimes ICD-10-CA provides an instruction to use an additional code to fully describe a person's condition. The "use additional code" instruction is provided to identify associated factors in a condition, such as infecting organism in local infections, functional activity in neoplasia, underlying cause in organic mental disorders and conditions resulting from toxic agents. In most cases, the "use additional code" instruction leads to an asterisk code. In other situations, ICD-10-CA provides an instruction to "code separately" a condition that may occur in combination with another condition. When the instruction is "use additional code", it is mandatory that the additional code be assigned when applicable with the exception of codes in the B95–B97 block. When the instruction is "code separately" the additional code must be assigned when the condition affects the care of the patient.

Example:

Agranulocytic mucositis. "Use additional code" instruction, it is mandatory to assign D70.0.	K12.3 Oral mucositis (ulcerative) D70.0 Neutropenia

Example:

Urinary tract infection due to E. coli.	N39.0	Urinary tract infection, site not specified
"Use additional code" instruction, it is optional to assign B96.2.	B96.2	Escherichia coli [E. coli] as the cause of diseases classified to other chapters

Example:

Congestive heart failure with Type 1 diabetes.	I50.0	Congestive heart failure
	E10.52	Type 1 diabetes mellitus with certain circulatory complications
"Code separately" instruction, I50.0 must be assigned when it affects the care of the patient.		

Other Circumstances for Use of Multiple Codes

When the classification of multiple conditions is not provided for in one of the circumstances described above, the coder must assign multiple codes to fully describe the person's condition. Each condition is coded separately whether they are related conditions or not.

Example:

Congestive heart failure and coronary artery disease.	I50.0	Congestive heart failure
	I25.19	Atherosclerotic heart disease of unspecified type of vessel, native or graft

Example:

Ruptured berry aneurysm. COPD.	I60.7	Subarachnoid haemorrhage from intracranial artery, unspecified
	J44.9	Chronic obstructive pulmonary disease, unspecified

UNCONFIRMED DIAGNOSES

When no definite diagnosis has been established by the end of a health care encounter, then the information recorded by the physician that permits the greatest degree of specificity about the condition that necessitated the encounter is coded. [CIHI, Canadian Coding Standards for v2009, p22] When a patient is transferred to another facility for further diagnostic work up and treatment, the diagnosis at the transferring institution is coded to what was known at the time of transfer.

When the main condition is recorded by the physician as "suspected", "questionable", "probable", "query", "rule out", etc. on discharge, and there is no further information or clarification, the suspected diagnosis must be coded as if established. This is based on the theory that the diagnostic and therapeutic interventions would have addressed this condition even though a final determination was not made. To identify a condition as unconfirmed, a prefix of "Q" is placed before the ICD-10-CA code.

Example:

Chest pain. ? MI.	R07.4	Chest pain, unspecified
What is known about this case is "chest pain"; the underlying condition is recorded as a "query", i.e. a "Q" is placed before the code.	Q I21.9	Acute myocardial infarction, unspecified

Example:

| Probable ovarian cyst. | Q N83.2 Other and unspecified |
| In this case the condition is recorded as "probable" and there is no further information or clarification. | ovarian cysts |

The use of the terms "rule out" and "ruled out" in the documentation can be confusing. The term "rule out" is interpreted to mean the diagnosis is still considered to be possible. A final diagnosis recorded as "rule out" (sometimes written as R/O) is coded as if established as described above (i.e. with a "Q" placed before the code). The term "ruled out" is interpreted to mean that diagnostic interventions have excluded the diagnosis as a possibility and it is not coded (see Chapter 25 for direction on coding these cases).

> Code conditions recorded as "rule out" (R/O) as if established and place a "Q" in front of the code. Do not code conditions described as "ruled out".

ACUTE AND CHRONIC CONDITIONS

When a condition is described as being both acute (or subacute) and chronic, and ICD-10-CA provides separate categories or subcategories for each, but not a combination category, the code for the acute condition is assigned. [ICD-10 Vol 2, p111] Assignment of an additional code to describe the chronic condition is optional unless each condition is treated separately. When a combination category is provided, only one code is assigned.

Example:

| Acute and chronic cholecystitis. | K81.0 Acute cholecystitis |
| A combination code is not provided, code the acute condition; assignment of a code for the chronic condition is optional. | K81.1 Chronic cholecystitis (optional) |

Example:

| Acute exacerbation of chronic obstructive bronchitis. | J44.1 Chronic obstructive pulmonary disease with acute exacerbation, unspecified |
| A combination code is provided. | |

SEQUELAE OF CERTAIN CONDITIONS

When a person is admitted for treatment or investigation of a sequelae (lingering or resulting condition) of a disease that is no longer present, a code for the current problem is assigned. These conditions are frequently documented as "old", "late effect of" or "due to previous". ICD-10-CA provides categories to provide further information about conditions which are no longer present but are the cause of the current problem undergoing treatment or investigation. These are assigned as additional codes and include:

- B90–B94   Sequelae of infectious and parasitic diseases
- E64.–   Sequelae of malnutrition and other nutritional deficiencies
- E68   Sequelae of hyperalimentation
- G09   Sequelae of inflammatory diseases of central nervous system
- I69.–   Sequelae of cerebrovascular disease
- O97.–   Death from sequelae of direct obstetric causes
- T90–T98   Sequelae of injuries, of poisoning and of other consequences of external causes
- Y85–Y89   Sequelae of external cause of morbidity and mortality.

The use of these codes is optional and are assigned only when their presence adds significant clarification. When the sequelae code is assigned, it is sequenced after the code for the current problem. When a specific lasting condition is not documented and the diagnosis is simply recorded as "late effect" of a previous condition or "old", the sequelae code may be assigned on its own when the circumstances described in the record merit this code assignment. Sequelae codes are located in the alphabetical index under the lead term "sequelae".

Example:

| Dysphasia due to old cerebral infarction. | R47.0 | Dysphasia and aphasia |
| | I69.3 | Sequelae of cerebral infarction |

Example:

| Old CVA. | I69.4 | Sequelae of stroke, not specified as haemorrhage or infarction |

USE OF SYMPTOM CODES

Codes for symptoms or signs which are characteristic of the diagnosis and, therefore, implicit in the diagnosis are not assigned; only the code for the underlying condition is assigned. For example, R10.0 *Acute abdomen* is not assigned in a patient with a diagnosis of acute appendicitis.

> Do not assign codes for symptoms or signs which are characteristic of the diagnosis.

Complete Exercise 2.4

Chapter 2   Exercise 2.1

ICD-10-CA

OBJECTIVE:

Explain ICD-10-CA.

INSTRUCTIONS:

① Read the *Introduction, General Principles of ICD-10-CA* and *Structure and Presentation of ICD-10-CA* sections of this Chapter.

② Answer each of the following:

1. What is ICD-10?

2. What is ICD-10-CA?

3. What is a classification system?

4. What are the elements of arrangement in the ICD-10-CA?

5. What is the distinction between a statistical classification and a nomenclature?

6. In ICD-10-CA, why are some disease entities given a separate title and code (i.e. category)?

7. How are conditions of "less" importance or frequency managed in ICD-10-CA?

8. What is meant by the term "axis"?

9. What is the axis of ICD-10-CA?

10. How are the categories identified in ICD-10-CA?

11. When can three-character codes be used alone?

12. Explain the meaning and significance of "residual categories".

13. Why is it important for coders to refer to the beginning of a chapter or block before confirming their code selection?

Chapter 2 — Exercise 2.2

ICD-10-CA

OBJECTIVE:

Use the ICD-10-CA alphabetical index to accurately locate the ICD-10-CA code for diagnostic statements.

INSTRUCTIONS:

① Read the *Alphabetical Index* section of this chapter and the section in the ICD-10-CA entitled *Conventions Used in the Alphabetical Index*.

② For each of the following statements, identify:
   - whether the statement is a diagnostic statement or a procedural statement
   - If it is a diagnostic statement, further identify:
      - the lead term for locating the statement in the alphabetical index
      - the secondary term(s) in the statement.

③ Conduct a search of the alphabetical index (binoculars #1) using the appropriate lead terms and secondary terms and identify:
   - the code as supplied by the alphabetical index
   - any special instructions, notes, nonessential modifiers, etc.

④ Review the table of contents for ICD-10-CA and note which chapter in ICD-10-CA you would expect the code to be found.

⑤ Record your responses in the spaces provided. Complete the first line only if it is a procedural statement.

Example: Bacterial meningitis (streptococcal).

For the above statement, identify:	Response
Diagnostic or procedural statement?	Diagnostic
Lead term	Meningitis
Secondary terms	Bacterial Streptococcal
Code supplied by the alphabetical index	G00.2 G00.9 is not correct as you have been provided with more specific information indicating the type of bacteria.
Special instructions, notes, nonessential modifiers, etc.	"acute" is a nonessential modifier following the secondary term "Streptococcal"
Chapter where you would expect the code to be found	Chapter VI - Diseases of the nervous system (G00-G99)

1. Chronic sinusitis.

For the above statement, identify:	Response
Diagnostic or procedural statement?	
Lead term	
Secondary terms	
Code supplied by the alphabetical index	
Special instructions, notes, nonessential modifiers, and other discoveries.	
Chapter where you would expect the code to be found	

2. Subdural hematoma.

For the above statement, identify:	Response
Diagnostic or procedural statement?	
Lead term	
Secondary terms	
Code supplied by the alphabetical index	
Special instructions, notes, nonessential modifiers, and other discoveries.	
Chapter where you would expect the code to be found	

3. Embolic infarction of spleen.

For the above statement, identify:	Response
Diagnostic or procedural statement?	
Lead term	
Secondary terms	
Code supplied by the alphabetical index	
Special instructions, notes, nonessential modifiers, and other discoveries	
Chapter where you would expect the code to be found	

4. Hypertrophic eyelid.

For the above statement, identify:	Response
Diagnostic or procedural statement?	
Lead term	
Secondary terms	
Code supplied by the alphabetical index	
Special instructions, notes, nonessential modifiers, and other discoveries.	
Chapter where you would expect the code to be found	

5. Engorged breast.

For the above statement, identify:	Response
Diagnostic or procedural statement?	
Lead term	
Secondary terms	
Code supplied by the alphabetical index	
Special instructions, notes, nonessential modifiers, and other discoveries.	
Chapter where you would expect the code to be found	

6. Fibrocystic disease of breast.

For the above statement, identify:	Response
Diagnostic or procedural statement?	
Lead term	
Secondary terms	
Code supplied by the alphabetical index	
Special instructions, notes, nonessential modifiers, and other discoveries.	
Chapter where you would expect the code to be found	

7. Transurethral prostatectomy.

For the above statement, identify:	Response
Diagnostic or procedural statement?	
Lead term	
Secondary terms	
Code supplied by the alphabetical index	
Special instructions, notes, nonessential modifiers, and other discoveries.	
Chapter where you would expect the code to be found	

8. Bleeding duodenal ulcer.

For the above statement, identify:	Response
Diagnostic or procedural statement?	
Lead term	
Secondary terms	
Code supplied by the alphabetical index	
Special instructions, notes, nonessential modifiers, and other discoveries.	
Chapter where you would expect the code to be found	

9. Complete vaginal hysterectomy with bilateral salpingo-oophorectomy.

For the above statement, identify:	Response
Diagnostic or procedural statement?	
Lead term	
Secondary terms	
Code supplied by the alphabetical index	
Special instructions, notes, nonessential modifiers, and other discoveries.	
Chapter where you would expect the code to be found	

10. Internal thrombosed hemorrhoids.

For the above statement, identify:	Response
Diagnostic or procedural statement?	
Lead term	
Secondary terms	
Code supplied by the alphabetical index	
Special instructions, notes, nonessential modifiers, and other discoveries.	
Chapter where you would expect the code to be found	

11. Cardiac pacemaker status.

For the above statement, identify:	Response
Diagnostic or procedural statement?	
Lead term	
Secondary terms	
Code supplied by the alphabetical index	
Special instructions, notes, nonessential modifiers, and other discoveries.	
Chapter where you would expect the code to be found	

12. Acute upper respiratory infection with influenza.

For the above statement, identify:	Response
Diagnostic or procedural statement?	
Lead term	
Secondary terms	
Code supplied by the alphabetical index	
Special instructions, notes, nonessential modifiers, and other discoveries.	
Chapter where you would expect the code to be found	

13. Urinary tract infection due to E coli.

For the above statement, identify:	Response
Diagnostic or procedural statement?	
Lead term	
Secondary terms	
Code supplied by the alphabetical index	
Special instructions, notes, nonessential modifiers, and other discoveries.	
Chapter where you would expect the code to be found	

14. Acute suppurative mastoiditis with subperiosteal abscess.

For the above statement, identify:	Response
Diagnostic or procedural statement?	
Lead term	
Secondary terms	
Code supplied by the alphabetical index	
Special instructions, notes, nonessential modifiers, and other discoveries.	
Chapter where you would expect the code to be found	

Chapter 2 — Exercise 2.3

ICD-10-CA

OBJECTIVE:
Apply conventions used in ICD-10-CA tabular list.

INSTRUCTIONS:

① Read the section in the ICD-10-CA entitled *Conventions Used in the Tabular List of Diseases*.

② For each of the following statements, provide the requested information by consulting the specific entry in the Tabular List.

---

1. What is excluded from C00 *Malignant neoplasm of the lip*?

2. At D55.2 *Anaemia due to disorders of glycolytic enzymes*, can a diagnosis simply stated as "Anemia" be classified to this category? Why or why not?

3. Which of the following codes would you assign to a diagnosis stated as "SCID"? Why?

    a. D81.0
    b. D81.8
    c. D81.9

4. What is the inclusion term in the entry for G51.0 *Bell's Palsy*?

5. What four conditions are included in L05 *Pilonidal cyst*?

6. At N77.0 *Ulceration of vulva in infectious and parasitic diseases classified elsewhere*, why is herpes simplex enclosed in square brackets?

7. At N28.1 *Cyst of kidney, acquired* what do the words "multiple" and "solitary" in the inclusion term signify for the coder?

8. At M54.0 *Panniculitis affecting regions of neck and back*, explain the meaning of "NOS" in the "excludes" list as it applies in this case.

9. At J20 *Acute Bronchitis*, there is both an inclusion note and an exclusion note relating to the age of 15. Explain how you would use these notes.

10. The category J86 *Pyothorax* contains the instruction "Use additional code (B95–B97) to identify infectious agent". Explain this instruction. Which code is the primary code?

11. In the previous question, how should the coder reconcile the instruction and the "excludes" note?

12. At M21.54 *Acquired clawhand, clubhand, clawfoot and clubfoot, hand*, do all conditions have to be present in order to use this code? Explain the convention used in this code.

Chapter 2 — Exercise 2.4

ICD-10-CA

OBJECTIVE:

Apply ICD-10-CA coding guidelines to correctly select ICD-10-CA codes.

INSTRUCTIONS:

① Read the the section in the ICD-10-CA entitled *Basic Coding Guidelines*. You can locate this by opening the table of contents and double clicking on this text.

② For each of the following statements, apply the coding guidelines to determine the correct ICD-10-CA code.

③ Note the applicable coding guideline in each situation.

	Code
1. Right inguinal hernia and nongangrenous obstruction of bowel. GUIDELINE:	
2. Myelopathy due to displaced cervical intervertebral disc. GUIDELINE:	
3. Hypertension with subarachnoid hemorrhage from ruptured vertebral artery aneurysm. GUIDELINE:	
4. Diaphragmatic hernia with gastroesophageal reflux. GUIDELINE:	

	Code
5. Right lower quadrant abdominal pain, probable ruptured corpus luteum cyst. GUIDELINE:	
6. Non-Q wave myocardial infarction, NSTEMI, coronary artery disease. GUIDELINE:	
7. Infertility due to tubal occlusion from old tuberculosis. GUIDELINE:	
8. Instability left knee; patient had a skiing injury five years ago. GUIDELINE:	
9. Late effects of poliomyelitis. GUIDELINE:	
10. Dysuria from urinary tract infection due to E. coli. GUIDELINE:	

Chapter 3

CCI

- Introduction
- General principles of CCI
- Structure and presentation of CCI
- Locating codes in CCI
- Intervention attributes
- Application of CCI

INTRODUCTION

The *Canadian Classification of Health Interventions* (CCI) has been in use in Canada as the national standard for classification of health care interventions since April, 2001. The term "intervention" is used instead of "procedure" in the title of the classification to reflect its broad scope across the continuum of health services. The CCI contains a comprehensive list of diagnostic, therapeutic, and support interventions (approximately 18,000 codes).

The definition of "health care intervention" as used in CCI is "A service performed for (or on behalf of) a client whose purpose is to improve or promote health, or to alter or diagnose the course of a disease/health condition."

As in ICD-10-CA, the **tabular list** is the classification itself and is a listing of intervention codes in alphanumeric order. It also includes several diagrams to assist in code selection. The **alphabetic index** is a listing of interventions, in alphabetic order, leading to the codes in the tabular list. General and specific coding guidelines, instructions and information about CCI can be found at the beginning of the classification under the section entitled "Introduction to CCI". You can locate this by opening the Table of Contents and double clicking on this text.

The CCI is dynamic and expandable which means that it can be updated on a regular basis to accommodate changes in practice and technologies used to perform various interventions. Blocks of codes have been reserved to allow for future growth.

GENERAL PRINCIPLES OF CCI

The CCI utilizes a code-building logic within a multi-axial framework. The code structure is designed to identify different criteria (axes) within one code. Theoretically, a coder could "build" a code by selecting a component from each of the axes. However, this is not the intended use of CCI. The tabular list of CCI provides only those codes that describe interventions that are meaningful, valid, and relevant within the continuum of health service. However, recognition of the code-building logic and an understanding of the definitions used within each axis of CCI will enhance the coder's proficiency.

The guiding principles used to assist in the development of CCI form the basis of its key features. These are described in detail in the section entitled "Guiding Principles" within the "Introduction to CCI" found at the beginning of CCI.

Complete Exercise 3.1

STRUCTURE AND PRESENTATION OF CCI

ORGANIZATION OF CCI

CCI is organized into sections (chapters) which identify broad types of interventions based on the primary intent of the intervention. The first digit of a CCI code represents the section. The sections of CCI are listed in Table 3.1.

ORGANIZATION OF CCI	
Section	Content
1	Physical/Physiological **Therapeutic** Interventions
2	**Diagnostic** Interventions
3	Diagnostic **Imaging** Interventions
4	Not in use
5	**Obstetrical** and **Fetal** Interventions
6	**Cognitive, Psychosocial** and **Sensory** Diagnostic and Therapeutic Interventions
7	**Other** Healthcare Interventions
8	Therapeutic Interventions Strengthening the **Immune System** and/or **Genetic Composition**

Table 3.1

The emphasis of this textbook is on sections 1, 2, 3 and 5.

Complete Exercise 3.2

Sections 1 to 3 are further subdivided according to body system or anatomy. The remaining sections are subdivided as appropriate for the content of the section. These subdivisions form the second part of a CCI code. Table 3.2 shows the subdivisions of each section and the corresponding character range.

SUBDIVISIONS OF THE SECTIONS IN CCI	
CCI Section	**Character Range**
Section 1 – Physical/Physiological **Therapeutic** Interventions	
Therapeutic interventions on the nervous system	1.AA–1.BZ
Therapeutic interventions on the eye and ocular adnexa	1.CC–1.CZ
Therapeutic interventions on the ear and mastoid (process)	1.DA–1.DZ
Therapeutic interventions on the orocraniofacial region	1.EA–1.FX
Therapeutic interventions on the respiratory system	1.GA–1.GZ
Therapeutic interventions on the cardiovascular system	1.HA–1.LZ
Therapeutic Interventions on the lymphatic system	1.MA–1.MZ
Therapeutic interventions on the digestive and hepatobiliary tracts and other sites within the abdominal cavity NEC	1.NA–1.OZ
Therapeutic interventions on the genitourinary system	1.PB–1.RZ
Therapeutic interventions on the musculoskeletal system	1.SA–1.WZ
Therapeutic interventions on the skin, subcutaneous tissue and breast	1.YA–1.YZ
Therapeutic interventions on the body NEC	1.ZX–1.ZZ
Section 2 – **Diagnostic** Interventions	
Diagnostic interventions on the nervous system	2.AA–2.BX
Diagnostic interventions on the eye and ocular adnexa	2.CC–2.CZ
Diagnostic interventions on the ear and mastoid (process)	2.DA–2.DZ
Diagnostic interventions on the orocraniofacial region	2.EA–2.FY
Diagnostic interventions on the respiratory system	2.GE–2.GZ
Diagnostic interventions on the cardiovascular system	2.HA–2.LZ
Diagnostic interventions on the lymphatic system	2.MA–2.MZ
Diagnostic interventions on the digestive and hepatobiliary tracts and other sites within the abdominal cavity NEC	2.NA–2.OZ
Diagnostic interventions on the genitourinary system	2.PB–2.RZ
Diagnostic interventions on the musculoskeletal system	2.SA–2.WZ
Diagnostic interventions on the skin, subcutaneous tissue and breast	2.YA–2.YZ
Diagnostic interventions on the body system NEC	2.ZZ
Section 3 – Diagnostic **Imaging** Interventions	
Diagnostic imaging interventions on the nervous system	3.AF–3.AW
Diagnostic imaging interventions on the eye and ocular adnexa	3.CA–3.CZ
Diagnostic imaging interventions on the ear and mastoid (process)	3.DL–3.DZ
Diagnostic imaging interventions on the orocraniofacial region	3.EA–3.FY
Diagnostic imaging interventions on the respiratory system	3.GE–3.GY

CCI Section	Character Range
Section 3 – Diagnostic Imaging Interventions (continued)	
Diagnostic imaging interventions on the cardiovascular system	3.HA–3.LZ
Diagnostic imaging interventions on the lymphatic system	3.ML–3.MZ
Diagnostic imaging interventions on the digestive and hepatobiliary tracts and other sites within the abdominal cavity NEC	3.NA–3.OZ
Diagnostic imaging interventions on the genitourinary system	3.PB–3.RZ
Diagnostic imaging interventions on the musculoskeletal system	3.SC–3.WZ
Diagnostic imaging interventions on skin, subcutaneous tissue and breast	3.YL–3.YZ
Diagnostic imaging interventions on the body NEC	3.ZA–3.ZZ
Section 5 – Obstetrical and Fetal Interventions	
Antepartum interventions	5.AB–5.CA
Interventions on the fetus	5.FD–5.FT
Interventions during labour and delivery	5.LB–5.MD
Postpartum interventions	5.PB–5.PD
Section 6 – Cognitive, Psychosocial and Sensory Diagnostic and Therapeutic Interventions	
Therapeutic interventions for mental health and addictions	6.AA
Therapeutic interventions for interpersonal relationships	6.DA
Therapeutic interventions for cognition and learning	6.KA
Therapeutic interventions for communication	6.LA
Therapeutic interventions for hearing	6.PA
Therapeutic interventions for voice	6.RA
Therapeutic interventions for sight and other senses NEC	6.TA
Diagnostic and therapeutic interventions for motor and living skills	6.VA
Section 7 – Other Healthcare Interventions	
Personal care healthcare interventions	7.SC
Environmental healthcare interventions	7.SE
Service healthcare interventions	7.SF
Support activity healthcare interventions	7.SJ
Promoting health & preventing disease healthcare interventions	7.SP
Section 8 – Therapeutic Interventions Strengthening the Immune System and/or Genetic Composition	
Therapeutic interventions strengthening the immune system and/or genetic composition	8.AA–8.ZZ

Table 3.2

CODE STRUCTURE

The multi axial framework on which a CCI code is built consists of 6 fields. The fields contain alpha and/or numeric characters separated by decimals and hyphens. The potential code length is 10 characters. The first five characters (fields 1 to 3) make up what is called the **rubric** and describe **what** is being done. The remaining characters are the **qualifiers** (fields 4 to 6) which describe **how** the intervention is done. The rubrics are the most stable part of the code and will not change much over time, but the qualifiers are very dynamic as operative techniques and devices change with advancements in medical science and technology. The 6 fields of the code are as illustrated in Table 3.3.

CCI CODE STRUCTURE					
FIELD 1	**FIELD 2**	**FIELD 3**	**FIELD 4**	**FIELD 5**	**FIELD 6**
A	AA	AA	AA	BB	B
Section	Group	Intervention	Qualifiers		

Table 3.3   **A** = Alpha/Numeric   **B** = Alpha/Numeric or Blank

FIELD 1 **Section**   Contains **one character** which represents the CCI section identifying the broad types of interventions as described in Table 3.1.

FIELD 2 **Group**   Contains **two characters** which identify a related grouping. In sections 1 to 3, the groupings represent body system or anatomical site. In the other sections the groups represent subdivisions as appropriate for the content of the section. The groups are listed under each section shown in Table 3.2.

FIELD 3 **Intervention** Contains **two characters** which identify a generic type of intervention appropriate for each section. For example, organ removal is a type of intervention found in section 1 and it is not found in any other section. Psychological counselling is found in section 6 and no other. A list of the contents of this field and intervention definitions can be found in Appendix A under **Intervention Definitions** in CCI. It is important to refer to these definitions regularly.

FIELD 4 **Qualifier 1**   Contains **two characters**, the meanings of which are section-dependent. In section 1, 2 and 3, the two characters relate to the approach or technique used (e.g. 1.OD.89.^^ *Excision total, gallbladder*). In sections 1 and 2, the most common two-character combinations will quickly become apparent to the coder such as:
- open (e.g. LA)
- endoscopic through a natural orifice (e.g. BA)
- endoscopic percutaneous (DA)
- percutaneous needle (HA)

In other sections, the characters have discrete meanings appropriate for the section. For example, VA in section 3 identifies x-rays in which no contrast medium is used. A detailed list of the contents of field 4 can be found in Appendix A in CCI.

FIELD 5	Qualifier 2	Contains **two characters**, the meanings of which are section dependent. Sometimes this field is not required and it is left blank. When this field is not required but a character is required in field 6, field 5 is filled with XX. In section 1, 2 and 5, the characters relate to devices or agents used. When the characters relate to agents, the field contains an alpha and a numeric character. For an example, look at 1.AA.35.^^ *Pharmacotherapy (local), meninges and dura mater of brain*. When the characters relate to a device, the field contains two alpha characters. For an example, look at 1.EB.74.^^ *Fixation, zygoma*. In section 6, the characters refer to a method or tool and in section 8, the characters refer to agents.
FIELD 6	Qualifier 3	Contains **one character**, the meaning of which is section dependent. This qualifier is applicable to section 1 and 8 only. Sometimes this field is not required and the field is left blank. In section 1, the character relates to tissue used. For an example, look at 1.PC.85.LA-XX-J *Transplant, kidney, using living donor (allogenic or syngeneic) kidney* and 1.PC.85.LA-XX-K *Transplant, kidney, using deceased donor kidney*. In section 8, the character refers to a type, group or strain of an organism.

The code format includes all six fields (10 characters) which, for presentation purposes only, are shown with a decimal after fields 1, 2 and 3 and a hyphen between fields 4, 5 and 6. All codes contain, as a minimum, information in fields 1 to 4. Where fields 5 and 6 are not applicable, there is no character filling; these fields are left blank. In this text, the symbol "^^" indicates an incomplete CCI code.

> As a minimum, complete fields 1 to 4 for all CCI codes. Complete fields 5 and 6 whenever applicable. In other words, complete all fields applicable to a given intervention.

Example: 1.YM.89.LA *Excision total, breast, using open approach*					
FIELD 1	FIELD 2	FIELD 3	FIELD 4	FIELD 5	FIELD 6
Section	Group	Intervention	Qualifiers		
1	YM	89	LA	blank	blank

1	=	Physical/physiological therapeutic intervention
YM	=	Breast
89	=	Total Excision
LA	=	Open approach, no device and no tissue

Example: 1.YM.89.LA-XX-A *Excision total, breast, using open approach and autograft*

FIELD 1	FIELD 2	FIELD 3	FIELD 4	FIELD 5	FIELD 6
Section	Group	Intervention	\multicolumn{3}{c}{Qualifiers}		
1	YM	89	LA	XX	A

- 1 = Physical/physiological therapeutic intervention
- YM = Breast
- 89 = Total Excision
- LA = Open approach
- XX = Blank (no device used)
- A = Autograft

Example: 2.YM.71.LA *Biopsy, breast NOS, incisional biopsy*

FIELD 1	FIELD 2	FIELD 3	FIELD 4	FIELD 5	FIELD 6
Section	Group	Intervention		Qualifiers	
2	YM	71	LA	blank	blank

- 2 = Diagnostic Intervention
- YM = Breast
- 71 = Biopsy
- LA = Open approach, no device.

Example: 3.YM.10.VA *Xray, breast, without contrast*

FIELD 1	FIELD 2	FIELD 3	FIELD 4	FIELD 5	FIELD 6
Section	Group	Intervention		Qualifiers	
3	YM	10	VA	blank	blank

- 3 = Diagnostic Imaging Intervention
- YM = Breast
- 10 = X-ray
- VA = Without contrast

An understanding of the definitions used within each axis of CCI will enhance the coder's proficiency in code assignment. This is especially important for the definitions for field 3 (interventions) used in section 1. These definitions are frequently described as "generic interventions" which simply means that a general term is used to classify the **intent** of an intervention even when the intervention can be described using multiple other terms. For example, a partial mastectomy might also be described as:

- excision of a breast lesion
- partial excision of the breast
- subtotal mastectomy
- lumpectomy
- segmental excision of breast
- wedge resection of the breast
- quadrantectomy.

In all of these surgeries, the intent is to remove a part of the breast. CCI classifies these to the generic intervention of "partial excision" so that any partial excision of the breast is classified to this term regardless of how it is described in the documentation.

An alphabetical list of these definitions can be found in *Appendix A – CCI Code Structure* under **Intervention Definitions** in CCI. This can be accessed by double clicking on this text in the Table of Contents. A list in numeric order is provided as Appendix A at the **end of this text**. Coders must know and understand these definitions. *Appendix B – CCI Rubric Finder* provides grids which indicate the available interventions for each group within each section of CCI.

CCI contains diagrams to assist in selecting the appropriate anatomy site (field 2 in sections 1, 2 and 3). These diagrams can be located by clicking on *Diagrams in CCI* in the table of contents.

Complete Exercise 3.3

LOCATING CODES IN CCI

In CCI, the tabular list contains more inclusion terms than the alphabetic index. Therefore, the coding process is different from that used in ICD-10-CA in which the alphabetic index contains more inclusion terms. CCI codes are located by searching the tabular list first. This is done by using the advanced query (large, unnumbered binoculars icon) and entering the appropriate search terms. The challenge is in learning the appropriate words to use as search terms. For example, a search on the word cauterization in the advanced query will reveal some codes for sites where cauterization is a common intervention. However, a search on the word cauterization in the alphabetic index (binoculars #2 icon) will provide an instruction to "See Destruction, by site." For this reason new coders should first use the alphabetic index to develop their understanding of the generic intervention terms used in CCI as well as other aspects of the CCI code structure. Once you are comfortable with the terminology used in CCI, you can move on to using the advanced query.

As in ICD-10-CA, a search of the alphabetical index in CCI begins with identifying a lead term. However, unlike ICD-10-CA, this search will only lead to the rubric for the intervention (i.e. an incomplete code). The coder must then review the tabular list to select the appropriate qualifiers to complete the code.

> The alphabetic index provides incomplete codes. Coders must consult the CCI tabular list to obtain complete codes.

CONDUCTING A SEARCH USING LEAD TERMS AND SECONDARY TERMS

In Exercise 3.3, you were asked to review a procedural statement and identify the intervention being carried out. Identifying the intervention will, in most cases, determine the lead term. Lead terms generally reflect the **nature** or **intent** of the intervention. It may be helpful to consider what is being accomplished by the procedure. For example, consider the following intervention:

"Suture laceration of the face".

The intent of suturing a laceration is to repair the skin. Thus, "repair" is the lead term. The **secondary terms are most often anatomy sites** but may also be a device, the disorder (e.g. calculus), stages of pregnancy or other information pertaining to a section of CCI. In the example above, "skin" and "face" are the appropriate secondary terms. To locate the code for this intervention:

1. Click on the alphabetic index search button (binoculars #2)
2. Enter "repair" in the space provided for the lead term
3. Enter "skin face" in the space provided for the secondary terms (omit words such as "of", "and" and "the" as these are unnecessary)
4. Select "ok"

As in ICD-10-CA, you must step through the hits by clicking on the "Next partition hit" icon (small double arrows) until you come to the place where your lead term is the bolded term. Once you are at your lead term, step through the secondary terms using the "Next hit" icon (large double arrows) until one of the secondary terms is the first indented term under the lead term. When you step through the secondary terms correctly, you will arrive at:

Repair
- skin
- - face NEC 1.YF.80.^^ .

When a lead term cannot be found, review the clinical documentation to determine the generic nature or intent of the intervention. This requires the coder to be able to understand the documentation. Consulting the intervention definitions found in Appendix A of CCI will also be helpful. In some cases, alternate terms are provided in the alphabetic index as a cross reference to direct coders to a more appropriate lead term. Be prepared to refer to dictionaries, pathophysiology references, peers, surgical references, credible internet sites or the surgeon for help when the intent of a procedure is unclear.

Complete Exercise 3.4

COMPLETE THE CODE FROM THE TABULAR LIST

Once a term has been found, the coder **must** consult the tabular list to confirm correctness of choice by reading all instructional notes and inclusion/exclusion terms and to select the appropriate qualifier to complete the code.

As noted in Table 3.2, sections 1 to 3 are further sub-divided according to body system or anatomy and other sections are further subdivided as appropriate for the content of the section. These subdivisions are represented in field 2. The coder will find instructional notes, especially inclusion and exclusion notes, at the **beginning of any change in field 2.** Go to "Therapeutic Interventions on the Nervous System" in section 1 of CCI and find examples of notes found at the various levels of organization of the tabular list.

> Coders must regularly and frequently read information located at the beginning of each section and at the beginning of each change in field 2 of CCI.

When selecting the appropriate qualifiers to complete the CCI code, the coder must review the available choices provided in CCI. Knowing your choices will help you identify and locate the required information in the operation report. As a general rule, only one qualifier from a rubric is assigned to identify devices or techniques. When multiple qualifiers apply and there is no combination qualifier, the coder must choose the qualifier that is most significant for data collection. Facilities can advise CIHI of these cases for consideration in its classification maintenance. The exceptions to this rule are cases where specific instructions are provided permitting the use of multiple qualifiers or, in rare cases, where more than one operative approach is used.

Go to the "Introduction to CCI" and read the section "General Instructions on the Format and Structure of CCI", skipping over the section on "Attributes" at this point. Also read the section "How to Code With CCI".

CONDUCTING A SEARCH USING THE ADVANCED QUERY

Once you are familiar with the terminology and structure of CCI, you will be better able to search using the advanced query. The key is to locate the code in as few hits as possible. The usual description of an intervention is often effective (e.g. hysterectomy). However, a search using the generic intervention and the anatomy part (e.g. excision, total, uterus) requires a little more thinking, but will typically yield fewer hits. Remember to step through the hits until you come to the correct rubric and to read inclusion and exclusion notes carefully.

Complete Exercise 3.5

INTERVENTION ATTRIBUTES

In addition to the 10-character code, CCI provides a number of intervention attributes which contribute additional information related to the intervention. These attributes are not part of the code itself and are collected as separate data fields.

Intervention attributes do not apply to all CCI codes. Where intervention attributes have been identified as applicable to a rubric, an attribute box at the end of the rubric code is highlighted in yellow or pink. A grey attribute box indicates the attribute does not apply to the rubric. For example, at 1.TA.55.^^ *Removal of device, shoulder joint*, you see a yellow box containing the letter "S", a pink box containing the letter "L" and a grey box containing the letter "E". Click on the yellow and pink boxes to reveal their content. In sections 5 and 6 the "L" attribute is replaced by an "M" attribute. The content of attributes is described in Table 3.4.

CONTENT OF ATTRIBUTES	
Attribute	Meaning
S (Status)	- provides information about the circumstances of the intervention e.g. "Abandoned after Onset", "Revision" or "Staged"
L (Location)	- provides more anatomical detail e.g, "Left", "Right", or "Bilateral"
E (Extent)	- provides quantitative detail e.g. number of arteries bypassed or the size of calculi removed
M (Mode)	- provides information related to the way a particular intervention was delivered when anatomy site does not apply e.g. direct (in person), indirect (telemedicine)

Table 3.4

The requirement to assign attribute codes is determined at the national, provincial/ territory and local levels. Those that are mandatory at the national level are identified in pink and will contain a null value (0 to indicate that none of the attributes apply). The yellow S attributes are mandatory when they apply, but there is no null value (the attribute is left blank when none apply). New coders should include all intervention attributes (both those highlighted in yellow as well as pink) whenever they apply to help build this into the routine of the coding process and contribute to an understanding of interventions.

Read the section entitled "Attributes" in the "General Instructions on the Format and Structure of CCI". Also review Appendix C of CCI for more information about attributes.

> Assign attributes whenever they apply. Remember that pink attributes are mandatory at the national level and contain a null value.

SELECTING AN INTERVENTION ATTRIBUTE
To view the choices within an attribute, "click" on the attribute box and select the one that applies. Appendix C of CCI is provided for users of a paper version of the classification. The contents of the attribute box can be found by referencing the number that appears beside the attribute box in Appendix C. For example the content of a highlighted "S" box with the number "5" can be determined by locating S05 in Appendix C. The choices at S05 are "A- Abandoned after onset" and "R-Revision".

Complete Exercise 3.6

APPLICATION OF CCI

General and specific concepts for the use of CCI can be found under the section entitled "How to Code With CCI" within the introduction to CCI. Additional instructions and coding standards can be found in the *Canadian Coding Standards for Version 2009 ICD-10-CA and CCI*. The following will help to promote an understanding of CCI and assist in accurate code assignment.

USE OF COMPOSITE CODES VERSUS MULTIPLE CODES
Where possible, the CCI has attempted to eliminate the need for multiple codes to describe procedures commonly performed concomitantly. This is accomplished either at the rubric level, within qualifiers, with instructional notes, or in includes/excludes notes.

At the Rubric Level
In some circumstances, the entire rubric captures concomitant procedures. For example, a total mastectomy with reconstruction performed at the same episode is classified to 1.YM.90.^^ *Excision total with reconstruction, breast.*

Within Qualifiers
More commonly, qualifiers provide the means to identify a procedure performed in conjunction with another procedure. For example, repair of the knee joint is classified to 1.VG.80.^^ *Repair, knee joint*. When a meniscectomy is performed at the same time, a qualifier describing "with meniscectomy" is chosen.

Instructional Notes
Instructional notes often advise that certain procedures are included in a code for another procedure, implying a hierarchical structure. For example in the case of a synovectomy of the shoulder (1.TA.87.^^ *Excision partial, shoulder joint*) performed concomitantly with a ligament release of the shoulder (1.TA.80.^^ *Repair, shoulder joint*) the following instructional note is provided at 1.TA.87.^^:

> "Omit code: When any of the following interventions – ligament resection, repair or release -- are performed concomitantly with any type of joint excision(s) such as arthrectomy, chondrectomy, extraction (deposits, fragments, loose bodies), synovectomy (see 1.TA.80.^^)."

Where it has not been feasible to provide composite codes, an instructional "code also" note may be provided to advise coders to assign an additional code when another procedure was performed at the same time. These "code also" notes are not exhaustive and coders must assign multiple codes to completely describe an operative episode when a composite code or "code also" instruction is not provided.

Includes/Excludes Notes

Includes and excludes notes provide another example of the hierarchical nature of certain codes. Some procedures which are classified separately when performed alone may be listed as an excludes note when performed in combination with another procedure higher in the hierarchical structure and listed as an includes note at that procedure. Reduction with fixation of a fracture is an example of this.

> **Example:**
>
> 1.VQ.73.^^ Reduction, tibia and fibula
> Excludes: that with fixation, tibia and fibula (see 1.VQ.74.^^)
>
> 1.VQ.74.^^ Fixation, tibia and fibula
> Includes: Reduction with fixation, tibia and fibula
>
> Reduction of the tibia <u>without</u> fixation is classified to 1.VQ.73.^^. Reduction of the tibia <u>with</u> fixation is classified to 1.VQ.74.^^.

As in ICD-10-CA, interpretation of excludes notes can be tricky. In the above example, the exclude note directs a coder to another code and only one code is assigned. However, in some circumstances the exclude note can direct the coder to assign multiple codes. Specifically, it may mean that a code does not include the intervention described in the excludes note and when that procedure was performed as an additional procedure, it is coded separately.

> **Example:**
>
> 1.VQ.74.^^ Fixation, tibia and fibula
> Excludes: Fixation, head and neck of tibia and fibula (see 1.VG.74.^^)
>
> In this example, the exclude note serves as a warning that if it is the head and/or neck of the tibia and/or fibula undergoing fixation the correct code is 1.VG.74.^^. However, when both the shaft of the tibia and/or fibula as well as the head and/or neck of the tibia and/or fibula undergo fixation, codes from both rubrics are assigned.

Often excludes notes have nothing to do with combination or multiple code assignment at all. They may simply serve the purpose of warning the coder to not use a code for certain circumstances.

> **Example:**
>
> 1.PC.13.^^ Control of bleeding, kidney
> Excludes: that done by surgical repair (see 1.PC.80.^^)
>
> This "excludes note" advises the coder to not use 1.PC.13.^^ when bleeding of the kidney is stopped by repairing the kidney (e.g. with sutures or grafting)

Composite codes or the requirement to use multiple codes are frequently found in procedures of joints. The combination codes apply when multiple procedures are performed on the **same** joint (i.e. same anatomical site code). Multiple coding is required when procedures are performed on different joints (i.e. different anatomical site codes).

When the same procedure is performed at the same anatomical site **bilaterally**, the procedure is coded only once. Bilaterality is identified through the location attribute.

COMBINED DIAGNOSTIC AND THERAPEUTIC INTERVENTIONS

When an intervention is performed that has both diagnostic and therapeutic purposes, only the code indicating the therapeutic intervention is assigned. For example, a biopsy described as **excisional** or one in which an entire lesion is removed has both a diagnostic and therapeutic purpose. This is classified to a code from section 1, specifically *partial excision* of the site. A code from section 2 is not assigned.

Aspiration of fluids from a body cavity are considered to have both a therapeutic and diagnostic benefit. In these cases only the therapeutic intervention of *drainage* is assigned.

When a diagnostic intervention is encompassed in a therapeutic intervention at the same anatomy site and during the same operative episode, only the code for the therapeutic intervention is required. This is intended to minimize the data collection burden. However, facilities may choose to assign an additional code for the diagnostic intervention as required to meet their data reporting needs.

IMAGING INTERVENTIONS

The assignment of a code for imaging interventions when they are performed in conjunction with a therapeutic procedure is optional (with the exception of coronary angiograms which must be coded whenever they are performed). However in the early stages of learning, new coders are encouraged to code these because this will help develop an appreciation of the full range of diagnostic and therapeutic interventions in patient management.

INSERTION OF STENTS

While stents are usually inserted to permit drainage, they accomplish this by maintaining the patency of a tube, duct, or vessel and are classified to **dilation** of the applicable site.

Complete Exercise 3.7

THERAPY USING PHARMACEUTICAL AGENTS

Some therapeutic interventions involve the use of pharmacological agents. The type of pharmacological agent is classified in the qualifier field of the CCI codes using an alphanumeric combination. As these are therapeutic interventions, they are found in section 1 of CCI. Specifically, these are found in:

    1.^^.35.^^   Pharmacotherapy (local)
    1.ZZ.35.^^   Pharmacotherapy (systemic)

When classifying pharmaceuticals delivered via the vascular system, it can be confusing as to whether these are local or systemic. For CCI classification, when an agent is delivered via a venous approach, it is classified as systemic. When an agent is delivered via an arterial approach, it is classified as local.

> Classify agents delivered via a (an):
> - **venous** approach to Pharmacotherapy (**systemic**)
> - **arterial** approach to Pharmacotherapy (**local**).

Appendix D in CCI provides a list of the groups or subgroups of pharmacological agents. It serves as a useful reference for identifying broad groupings of various agents for selection of the appropriate code in the second qualifier. In many cases, the information from Appendix D is included in a pop-up note at an applicable code (pop-up notes can be revealed by clicking on the ++ symbol). Health care documentation will often provide only the brand name of certain agents. The coder may need to reference a drug book to find the generic name of the agent to determine the appropriate category for classification.

Complete Exercise 3.8

Chapter 3   Exercise 3.1

CCI

OBJECTIVE:

Describe CCI.

INSTRUCTIONS:

① Read the "Guiding Principles" section within the "Introduction to CCI".

② Answer each of the following:

---

1. Name the organization that developed the CCI?

---

2. The CCI addresses the needs of various users across the health care continuum. Explain this statement.

---

3. Explain "service provider and service-setting neutral".

---

4. Suggest the meaning of "multi-axial" as it relates to the CCI.

5. Suggest the impact of the multi-axial nature of the CCI on data retrieval and analysis.

6. Explain "relevant" as it relates to the CCI.

7. Explain "dynamic and expandable" as it relates to the CCI.

8. When might diagnostic detail be included in the CCI?

Chapter 3 — Exercise 3.2

CCI

OBJECTIVE:

Predict the CCI section to which interventions are classified.

INSTRUCTIONS:

① For each of the following health care interventions, predict the CCI Section (1 - 8) in which the intervention would be classified. Use the Table 3.1 (page 3.2) as a reference.

	INTERVENTION	SECTION
1.	Appendectomy	
2.	Cholangiogram	
3.	Arthroscopy of the knee	
4.	Vasectomy	
5.	Episiotomy	
6.	ECG	
7.	Biopsy of the bladder	
8.	Study skills instruction	
9.	Digital examination of the prostate	
10.	Suture of laceration of scalp	
11.	MMR vaccination	
12.	Tamoxifen chemotherapy	
13.	Group psychotherapy	
14.	Laparoscopy	
15.	TUPR	
16.	Nutrition counseling	
17.	Ultrasound of the abdomen	
18.	Dental filling	

Chapter 3 — Exercise 3.3

CCI

OBJECTIVE:

Demonstrate the structure & presentation of sections 1 and 2 of CCI.

INSTRUCTIONS:
① For each of the following health care interventions, indicate:
   a) whether it is a therapeutic or diagnostic intervention
   b) the anatomical site
   c) the generic type of intervention being carried out (use the list of intervention definitions found in *Appendix A – CCI Code Structure* in the CCI).
   d) the approach (select one of the 4 common approaches described in field 4 on page 3.5)

---

1   Arthrotomy of right knee with total meniscectomy.

a)	Therapeutic/diagnostic	
b)	Anatomical site	
c)	Intervention	
d)	Approach	

2   Right frontal craniotomy with resection of osteoma of frontal bone.

a)	Therapeutic/diagnostic	
b)	Anatomical site	
c)	Intervention	
d)	Approach	

3   Esophagoscopy with biopsy of esophagus.

a)	Therapeutic/diagnostic	
b)	Anatomical site	
c)	Intervention	
d)	Approach	

4   Transurethral prostatic resection.

a)	Therapeutic/diagnostic	
b)	Anatomical site	
c)	Intervention	
d)	Approach	

Chapter 3 — Exercise 3.4

CCI

OBJECTIVE:

Use the CCI alphabetical index to determine the generic intervention for intervention statements.

INSTRUCTIONS:

① For each of the following intervention statements, identify the lead term (nature or intent) and secondary term (usually the anatomy site) and record it in the spaces provided.

② Conduct a search of your lead term in the alphabetical index (binoculars #2). Does the Index direct you to an alternate lead term? Record this instruction in the space provided.

③ Review the "Intervention Definitions" found in Appendix A of the CCI. Determine the CCI generic intervention applicable to the statement and record this in the space provided.

---

1   Partial gastrectomy.

Lead term	
Secondary term	
Alternate term direction?	
Generic Intervention	

2   Insertion coronary artery stent for dilation.

Lead term	
Secondary term	
Alternate term direction?	
Generic Intervention	

3   Laparotomy with partial resection of small intestine and end-to-end anastomosis.

Lead term	
Secondary term	
Alternate term direction?	
Generic Intervention	

4. Wide resection of basal cell carcinoma of the calf.

Lead term	
Secondary term	
Alternate term direction?	
Generic Intervention	

5. Freeing of adhesions of jejunum.

Lead term	
Secondary term	
Alternate term direction?	
Generic Intervention	

6. Transurethral removal of ureteral calculus.

Lead term	
Secondary term	
Alternate term direction?	
Generic Intervention	

7. Percutaneous transluminal balloon angioplasty, coronary artery.

Lead term	
Secondary term	
Alternate term direction?	
Generic Intervention	

8. Bilateral breast reduction.

Lead term	
Secondary term	
Alternate term direction?	
Generic Intervention	

9. Flushing of ventriculoperitoneal shunt.

Lead term	
Secondary term	
Alternate term direction?	
Generic Intervention	

10. Insertion, ureteral stent.

Lead term	
Secondary term	
Alternate term direction?	
Generic Intervention	

Chapter 3 — Exercise 3.5

CCI

OBJECTIVE:

Apply the tabular list in CCI

INSTRUCTIONS:

① In the CCI, read the section "General Instructions on the Format and Structure of CCI", skipping over the section on "Attributes". Also read the section "How to Code With CCI".

② Determine the correct CCI code for each of the following health care interventions. Record the code in the space provided. Try searching using both the alphabetical index (binoculars #2) and the Advanced Query (large, unnumbered binoculars).

③ Make note of any conventions, instructions or other notes you had to follow in order to arrive at the correct code.

	Code(s)
1. Laparoscopic appendectomy. NOTES:	
2. Excision branchial cleft fistula in neck. NOTES:	
3. Arthrotomy of right knee with partial patellectomy. NOTES:	

	Code(s)
4. Laser repair retinal detachment and scleral buckle. NOTES:	
5. Intracapsular cataract extraction with anterior chamber lens prosthesis. NOTES:	
6. Fasciotomy Dupuytren's contracture. NOTES:	
7. External closed reduction fracture, 3rd metacarpal. NOTES:	
8. Gastrectomy, partial, open, with esophagogastrostomy. NOTES:	

	Code(s)
9. Incision and drainage of abscess of face. NOTES:	
10. Fixation fractured mandible and maxilla with wire. NOTES:	

Chapter 3 — Exercise 3.6

CCI

OBJECTIVE:

Apply intervention attributes to CCI codes.

INSTRUCTIONS:

① Read the sections in the CCI manual related to intervention attributes.

② For each of the following health care interventions, use the advanced query or the alphabetical index to locate the correct CCI code and the applicable intervention attributes.

③ The shaded columns are provided for entering the attributes applicable to CCI codes. (S = status attribute, L = location attribute and E = extent attribute). When an attribute is available but not applicable, enter a dash (–). When no attribute is available, enter a slash (/).

	Codes	S	L	E
1. Laparoscopy with bilateral tubal ligation and division.				
2. Transurethral basket removal of 2.5 mm calculus, right ureter.				
3. Intraoperative T-tube cholangiogram.				
4. Secondary closure of operative wound of abdominal wall (7 days).				

	Codes	S	L	E
5. Esophagoscopy with biopsy of esophagus.				
6. Percutaneous transluminal balloon angioplasty, left coronary artery. Performed within 12 hours of presentation to hospital. Patient has STEMI, no thrombolysis, and no previous angioplasty.				

Chapter 3 — Exercise 3.7

CCI

OBJECTIVE:

Use the alphabetical index and the advanced query to assign the correct code from CCI.

INSTRUCTIONS:

① For each of the following health care interventions, determine the correct CCI code and the applicable intervention attributes. In each case, search using both the advanced query and the alphabetical index.

② Make note of any conventions, instructions, or other notes you had to follow in order to arrive at the correct code.

③ The shaded columns are provided for entering the attributes applicable to CCI codes. (S = status attribute, L = location attribute and E = extent attribute). If an attribute is available but not applicable, enter a dash (–). If no attribute is available, enter a slash (/).

	Code	S	L	E
1. Total abdominal hysterectomy with vaginal repair of cystocele and rectocele (sutures). NOTES:				
2. Burch suspension (abdominal vesicourethral fixation into Cooper's ligament using a ligature). NOTES:				
3. Excisional biopsy, lesion of skin of right calf with advancement flap closure. NOTES:				

	Code	S	L	E
4. Graft of defect in dura using fascia from patient's right thigh. NOTES:				
5. Excision malignancy left eyelid, partial thickness with composite graft reconstruction. NOTES:				
6. Release and transposition of ulnar nerve (open technique), left wrist. NOTES:				
7. Arthrotomy of right knee with total excision of right medial meniscus and patellar shaving. NOTES:				
8. Needle pleurocentesis. NOTES:				
9. Gastroscopy and laser optical biopsy of stomach. NOTES:				

	Code	S	L	E
10. Craniotomy and excision tumour of left parietal lobe with intraoperative microscope. NOTES:				
11. Bronchoscopy for inspection and bilateral bronchial washings. NOTES:				
12. MRI of right knee (no enhancement). NOTES:				
13. Ultrasound guided amniocentesis for chromosome analysis, single fetus. NOTES:				
14. Marriage therapy, individual, psychodynamic, short term, provided in person by a psychologist. NOTES:				
15. Diabetic diet counseling, one-on-one. NOTES:				
16. Tetanus booster injection, following puncture of left foot (< 5 cm) on rusty nail, cleansing and suture of injury. NOTES:				

Chapter 3 — Exercise 3.8

CCI

OBJECTIVE:

Classify administration of pharmaceutical agents.

INSTRUCTIONS:

① For each of the following health care interventions, determine the correct CCI code and the applicable intervention attributes. Try searching using both the advanced query and the alphabetical index.

② Make note of any conventions, instructions, or other notes you had to follow in order to arrive at the correct code.

③ Use Appendix D to confirm your selection.

④ The shaded columns are provided for entering the attributes applicable to CCI codes. (S = status attribute, L = location attribute and E = extent attribute). When an attribute is available but not applicable, enter a dash (–). When no attribute is available, enter a slash (/).

	Code	S	L	E
1. Single-vessel coronary artery balloon angioplasty with intracoronary infusion of Streptokinase; coronary angiograms via femoral artery. NOTES:				
2. Systemic (intravenous) chemotherapy with Tamoxifen. NOTES:				

	Code	S	L	E
3. Administration of analgesia via epidural catheter for postoperative pain control. NOTES:				
4. Irrigation of enterostomy using neomycin solution (per orifice). NOTES:				
5. Shampoo of scalp for pediculosis using Kwellada (lindane) shampoo. NOTES:				
6. Instillation of alpha-interferon into pleural cavity. NOTES:				